It Unveils

Only Truth

It Unveils

Only Truth

By Finnley R. Dean

Dedication

I want to thank everyone who believed in

me and my aspirations of publishing my first

book. The support of family and friends

means everything to me. Thank you.

Table Of Contents

Preface

This poetry book is a collection of 13 poems

that range in darkness in terms of death,

abuse, suicidal tendencies, and the theme of

crippling mental illness.

The Darkness of A Life Once Lived

I lie awake at night staring at the ceiling as if it had all the answers to my problems. Searching for something or someone to take the pain away Looking up as if it were the night sky and I was searching for God. Suddenly it faded to black as a teardrop slid down my face, letting my body consume itself in a black hole.

It was here, The Darkness I've tried to escape from, running and running till my feet bled and my breathing became shallow. My chest tight as if it were a hundred cinder blocks lying on it. I cry and scream inside, nothing escaping my mouth. Mouth sealed shut like it's super-glued together. My head swirls round and round like a carousel on an endless loop.

Tied down to my own bed, chained up with the shackles of my own illness. What can I do to stop the madness, something to make it end? I try to fight back, but my demons remain stronger each time. I splatter my blood across the pages looking for a release. Soaked the pages become. Red with depression, a disease of the mind, I see the escape from. Then I hear it, nothing but silence; so quiet you could hear every last breath and every single heartbeat that was.

Then it all stopped. I've indulged into myself and became The Darkness itself. I. Am gone...

A World Without

I look up at the sky and see nothing but grey clouds surrounding my very existence. A cruel, dull life that emits pain from every pore of my body. Sometimes I think about offing myself, so a world without me is something that I dream. No, I don't want to die but what other way can the agony subside.

I feel dread every day; small happiness is not enough to stay. Here on this place. Some say a world without isn't a world at all, but I can't see how when every day I fall. Down the rabbit I go I've made it my home, for all eternity because I want to be in a world without me.

The Noise That Screams

If you heard the noise, you knew you were sick. It was something so sinister that once heard it made you want to die instantly. I possess the curse of The Noise, you see, I can always hear it even when I sleep. I wish for silence in the echoes of its presence. Mental scarring leaving a visible one on my arms and thighs. I mark myself as The Noise tells me so. I paint the floors like a canvas with my own blood, yet no one knows a thing.

The Noise sometimes leads me to white walls and barred windows. Least there I'm safe, in a way. Other times it leads me down a path with nothing but straight razors and skin to look forward to. My body was its slave for it knew what to say to get me to obey. Empty promises of leaving me be. Lies of a conman it told.

JUST STOP ALREADY!! PLEASE GO AWAY!! I CAN'T LIVE

ANYMORE, I REFUSE TO STAY!!
The Noise That Screams won at the end
for I've ended my life before it had a
chance to begin.

A Burden I Secretly Bear

Something in me claw away at my
bones begging to be let out. Internal
screams echo throughout the chambers
of my flesh wanting to be unleashed as I
rip through my skin like wrapping paper
and left with the discarded remains
around me.

My brain is in constant flames, yet I still
smile. Somedays I wish it would burn

down leaving rubble and ash in its demise, but the flames still burn.

I feel love but also apathy evermore. Passion but also frustration.

It's like when I would take two magnets and try to get the backs of it to connect, you know it won't work but you try anyway and hope for a different result.

My Body is A Thorn Bush

Seeds of growth planted deep within the soil of one's heart

Bathed with somber tears of past despair

Yet outshone by beams of bright smiles and caring eyes

Stems rise and petals flourish but with it, grow thorns

Is it less exquisite though pain and sorrow riddle its very form?

One's distress does not devalue beauty of self nor worthiness of love.

The Bullets Were Laced

You had two right hands for you were his, he held the gun, but you pulled the trigger

Blind puppet with cut strings you are, why do you still dance with him though he walks in flames?

He, the man with many faces does not show his own till lights dim and you're left alone. He speaks with a forked tongue dripping with poison. His bullets are laced with the same.

If he points then he'll shoot, forever placing his blame on an innocent you.

In A Hidden Truth I Breathe

Even the hottest of summer nights felt cold with her presence

She was me in the flesh, but I was her in truth

I sought out life beyond rusted chains and twilight

Unknown to all, even the one I inhabit, she knows not who she will be

Because in a hidden truth, I breathe

If Leaves Be Crumbled

I fell apart again. The life with you I once knew has been tainted with the decisions of your dark nature. If I had not been controlled then only one of us would make it out alive, but alas sacrifices had to be made. My head swirled with thoughts of good times we shared but when the bad and awful outweighed the good, what was I to do besides stay? Though parts of me want to leave, I cannot ignore the latter that wants to work it out. But why such thoughts intertwine, well that's the million-dollar question, isn't it? Why stay when being crushed was our love language?

If hell was hot, then why did I freeze

If all I tried to do was heal, then how did I end up so broken.

A clock that doesn't tick

A feeling so sick

Sick of hurting

Sick of burning

Burning my skin cause you said you needed warmth

But all it did was leave me dying on the bathroom floor.

I Couldn't Swim

Let me lie in the creek where my body intertwines with the makings of naked ground.

Eyes red, soul dead

A feeling so empty, yet my mind overflows

Overflows, the moss grows

On my body so slow, no place I can go

To escape me

See, the creek was never a creek to begin

But my pained emotions controlling me till my end.

If God is Real, Then Maybe I'll Leave

O' water which flows through the hands of Gods, do you feel? Do you hurt? Do you love?

I only wish to be you for you go with wind and carry not which you can't control.

I will drown my sorrows with what you take away from here, then maybe one day I will be you.

I've let go and let water take me to the Gods.

A Love So Somber

O' how my tender soul yearns for your soft embrace.

Yet I wail for thy wicked tongue knows no mercy.

Will you ever love me? For my arms are reached for the slightest touch.

Will you ever care? For my heart bleeds out in my ever so fragile hands.

I beg for your love, yet you greet me with hate.

I beg for your kindness, yet you blackout in rage.

I know what I deserve, for you have stolen my smile.

I now sink into my own sorrow, for our love lost was my greatest tragedy.

Existence So Barren

I am nothingness in the form of a man

I am but a gather of cells

Who deserve none but death

The Light By Which I Stand

I've stood at this light post many times ago, and yet the feeling has remained the same. A presence of darkness and chaos overtook whatever used to feel right. Something about the light called to me in a way it hadn't for anyone else. We were synonymous with one another. I knew the brighter the light shone, the darker my soul would become, till there was nothing left of my former self.

I would stand by this light for it had been my company in times of sorrow, my guide in times of disarray, and my home when the one I knew was no longer the arms of acceptance and grace. I had sacrificed with my very own blood what it meant to be whole. I would no longer fear at the hands of humanity or would I ever grovel for the one thing I needed, love.

The ones who have done wrong upon me would suffer when near the light of pure vengeance. I would deliver the most powerful, evil of auras and devour their souls till nothing be left of them but an empty vessel, which carried it. I was no longer alone, I finally had family, the light I stood by many times ago.

Forevermore, we would be bonded with the darkness that consumed, for we were a force to be reckoned with among those who threatened us.

Afterword

Thank you for going on this journey with me inside the inner workings of my fucked-up brain.

Made in the USA
Columbia, SC
10 February 2021

31708673R00015